SOBER GHOST

JEFFREY SKINNER

POEMS

C&R Press
Conscious & Responsible

All Rights Reserved

Printed in the United States of America

First Edition
1 2 3 4 5 6 7 8 9

Selections of up to two pages may be reproduced without permission. To reproduce more than two pages of any one portion of this book, write to C&R Press publishers John Gosslee and Andrew Ibis.

Cover art by Laura Skinner

Copyright ©2024 Jeffrey Skinner
ISBN: 978-1-949540-45-1

C&R Press
Conscious & Responsible
crpress.org

For special discounted bulk purchases, please contact sales@crpress.org

SOBER GHOST

TABLE OF CONTENTS

I

Motion Against Ideas	12
Acceptance Speech	13
Love & Judgment	14
Lack of Perspective in an Early Drawing by One of My Daughters	16
Fields	17
The Channel Swimmer	18
Serpent Speak	19
A Marriage	20
Fronting	22
Pandemic	23
Wingsuit	24
The Mansion	26
Beginning with a Line by Van Gough	28
Beginning with a Line by J.A.	30
For My Brother Who Couldn't Stay	31
Without God Everything is Permitted	33
The Pearl	34
The Truth About Men	35
Shush	36
The Cloud	37
Satin	38
Blurb Cento	40
2022	41

II

In the Mind	45
Sober Ghost	46
How He Was Caught Up into Paradise, and Heard Unspeakable Words, which It Is Not Lawful for a Man to Utter	47
I'm Thinking of a Few Spectacular Ways to Die	48
Homage to Phil	49
(Words) (Music) (Money)	50
Insomnia	52
The Nighthawk	53
The Afterlife Has Already Begun	54
Mission Creep	56
I Said to My Friend Jimmy	60
On the Anniversary of My Sobriety	61
River, Bear	63
Prospero's Happiness	64
The Lion	66
It Was Later	67
Bearing Away	68
Even Night is Not Night Enough	69
Acknowledgments	72
Notes	73
About the Author	74

In memoriam Phil Levine

On the other hand, what I like my music to do to me is awaken the ghosts inside of me. Not the demons, you understand, but the ghosts.
—David Bowie

I have a piece of great and sad news to tell you: I am dead.
—Jean Cocteau

I

Motion Against Ideas

As for the idea we are all one
I notice cancer has removed pieces of Robert
But I am still whole.

I see a few people
Swimming in money, many others wading out
To supply drinks and sex.

The water's glassy blue. The many
Taken by the few. But I don't know them,
Don't fish, don't care.

It's cool to think our skulls
Contain sun, and moon, and stars, each head
A planetarium. The difference is

Heads switch off, quick,
Unlike stars. A new body, all new cells
Every seven years: Hell yes, why not! But, new

Cells that make us look older?
Your honor, entropy spreads us thin
And thinner. We'll soon be gloss.

Your honor, I move
We clear away ideas on both sides of the table
& wait wordless together

For as long as it takes
The soul to appear, then wait longer
For the maker of souls,

The maker of silence, the maker
Of words. Then listen,
And weep, and take notes.

Acceptance Speech

If no one else applies and it falls to me to confess all sin, I accept. Hammer, please. But that's so sere, don't you want to make poems that float, pushed back and forth in the air by like minds? No, thanks. Notice how long the Japanese maple hangs on to its leaves, brave cherry stars in weak sun. Notice the rain pelting you in nightmare has no substance, and stings nonetheless. Notice coincidence, a field of wild tulips opening at the same moment. If you look through time sideways some scenes show through: the suicide's pretty face, her car one with the tree on the Merritt Parkway. But, very far. Unreachable. Notice I haven't yet gotten to the sins.

Love & Judgment

Of course it was October I think maybe evening at least
That's when most things happened suddenly inside me
Happened on the skeleton of a bird at forest's edge
A crispy light in & around the scrubbed-clean matchstick bones
White now as god's teeth & as necessary, weightless

Nearly between thumb & index finger picking up the skull
A deep look my eyes so focused & sharp in those days
& the ant crawled out in tiny panic from eye socket
Onto my finger I dropped the skull though it hardly made
Any difference in hand's weight flung up ant flying off

Continued with purpose: forget the girl, what girl no matter
Walk through abandoned graveyard names all chewed
By time unreadable stone the smell of lake water
Floating just beyond opaque tannic black from surface
Down to mush black mud took off shoes walked out

A bit numb girl's face on surface broken on the way back
Picked up skull again blew hard through eyehole until clean
Dropped in shirt pocket light as origamied rolling paper
Remembered thinking skull white, & necessary
As god's teeth . . . Why necessary?   Carried the question

From forest & memory of some girl almost loved but what
Was love & judgment against nineteen years old
Everything weightless as a sparrow skull in pocket
Bobbing as I jogged through autumn the barred owls calling out
What do you know what do you know what do you know

Lack of Perspective in an Early Drawing by One of My Daughters

There's a small mountain of drugs in the frame
And next to it a smaller pile of me.
The drugs are about to be shoveled into me
By me, or maybe the shoveling has already begun.
Over the landscape, which I am refurbishing
To inscribe the echo of self, a sun-like yolk
Crayoned by one of my daughters.
Or is it a yolk-like sun? I was never sure
What my daughters had in mind. Then the ocean
To the right, its tiny blue and green curls,
Meticulous as the mind makes
Waves, and the wheat-blond sand, bordering.
Lastly a red towel, with a plastic
Shovel placed nearby. There, I think that's it.
Of course, my head is all wrong—big
As the ocean, big as the mountain of drugs,
Big as my daughters are small.
Who knew? Distant things on a plane
Must be drawn smaller, to mimic how the eye sees,
How time keeps shrinking what was, to is.

Fields

Many previous fields were blond with black stubble. Others, green with blue stubble & several horses. A black fence for acres. I take on the color of each field & stay alert for predators. Often at night the moon carves a furrow, as if a bowling alley for ghosts. When I have trouble sleeping, I go out & roll a few frames. Back in bed my hands glow faint silver. It's hard to meditate in the summer field because of wolves & bureaucrats, cicadas grinding grain into dry powder. In one field edged by roses & a marble goddess I was married. Then in another, by a farmer's rack of dead crows, divorced. This was the field where I learned what I would never do, never be. After that came the garden of what remained.

The Channel Swimmer

i.m. Leslie McGrath

I know someone entering non-being in the worst way
With lesions & tumors & denial & that pain unknowable
Until you know. But the channel between fast-forward dying
& the rest of us—you can't swim it this time of year

Or anytime, until it's your turn & you get greased up
& spit in your goggles & ease your body into the wet shock
& push off, your love following beside in a rowboat,
Rowing through the grief chop & handing you energy bars

& attaboys. And you think wrong thoughts but don't say
Them, like, *Is that the best you can do, love, really?*
You, the one not dying? Can't you join me, or at least
Take turns being me? An energy bar, really?

It's unfair, & the rest of us stand like lawn ornaments
Back on shore, one arm up & waving. Then slip
Into our cars & drive home because, well—what else
Can we do? No one we know has seen that other coast.

Serpent Speak

No one has asked me to apologize for breathing. But I know it's coming. Interesting what you see from the ground, right before they come at you with guns and pitchforks and stones: the comedy of each, laboring to appear taller than every other. And you see, close up, blood drain from wound and mouth, the hunger spark in the compound eyes of my friends, the blowflies. Everything comes to me, including death. I accept my station, I love my sleek life, even as I take care of your rats, your mice, which you don't credit. I don't care. Their diseases are delicious to me. Taunt me when I'm in a good mood and I'll move on. Corner me, and I have a serum. I will fuck you up.

A Marriage

Is this what it takes, she said
Holding the cat over the lit gas burner.
I had just returned from somewhere, possibly
The Yukon (I did lie), snow nestled
In the shearling trim of my suede coat.

I think we all need to put down our weapons,
I said. But you have caused a hurt
In me, she said, the balance between us askew,
Needing correction. The cat, closer
Now to the blue ring of flame, squirming.

The kitchen was oddly festive
Owing to the sun's entrance at such an angle
Even the salt and pepper shakers
Inked jaunty shadows. Perhaps festive
Is the wrong word. We were still, a long time.

Finally I could stand it no more
And took off my coat. Put down the animal,
I said. Let's discuss our feelings, which supposedly
Can heal. Then from outside came the pop
Of a streetlamp, a shower of glass.

I don't really care about cats, I said.
But it was dark and she was no longer there.

Fronting

Behind the façade of brick and cast iron there's a citizen garden, a cat asleep in a lettuce row. You can see through the windows, sometimes to the river. The river wanders, but at least it can taste, dimly, the salt of the afterlife. My façade is not so lucky. It feels like I come to each moment trailing worlds, like a circus that will not clean up after itself. Feels, but the science is missing. *Feels, it feels*... Oh Jeff (may I call you Jeff?) feelings don't care about your feelings. They are just tiny scuffs on time, the silvery vein running through the heart.

Pandemic

All over town we look to other towns. How you doin? You can't lift, or point a finger. Not allowed. When my personal head fell off, I thought—Ok, enough. That now is completely enough. Let us return to history, even that shitty road may be better. But no one hears air shushing from the public self, and no one reads the private self, that erasure poem. And so we gaze in at the lucky diners, licking rain from the window.

Wingsuit

For J.Y.B.

When I look out the window a flutter
And a beep: the heart backing up.
Brittle bones, evening hotel, red fade.
The mountain, shadowing the town.

The sun asks helmeted birds to enter.
I'm tall, let me help you with that;
I too was dropped into a sea of choppy air.
They wait on a ledge, check straps

And hand-folded parachutes.
They are in love with narrow entrance,
With being teased by death.
After the plunge, something like flying.

When I look down, my asshole buzzes.
It's mindless temptation,
It's the look on the end of the world's face,
It's the wonder drug of sheer drop.

If I repeat myself it's because I still want.
Listen, my one and only given name,
Nothing counts till you fall solo,
All in—the sky a packed gray doubt.

A patio faces the mountain ledge.
Over the town and river, a snake of fog.
I said to thin air, *Do I, do I, do I
Repeat myself?* Love hates being teased.

I looked into the sun. It's just a loud room.
No one sees the shadow on your face.
Real time begins with a cross and a leap.
I'm tall, let me help you with that.

The Mansion

I understand—the No One Cares billboard
Looms over the exit ramp; Nancy has lost her place
In her novel for the umpteenth time; the lab
Has dysplasia. Overhead, a species
Of blank Midwestern sky falls
Open like a journal you buy, full of hope,
Then leave in some drawer where it remains blank.
The universe is bored with my questions,
Finally. I knew it would happen
Though one is nevertheless taken by surprise.
So many in real pain remain silent.
Lonesome thing, in the forest, stay there!
Don't come out! You no longer fascinate.
I always begin by speaking
From exactly where I am. But then, you know—
The earth rotates, I am awash in lie
And pretension, waving a tiny flag at the moon.
If you make the song real it goes on
Singing itself, someone said, and that alone
Should be enough. Not like the repetition of money.
I buy the premise, but don't know where
It leaves me. Generally, we expect the poem
To circle back, to touch home base—
The breathless child crouching by the willow,
Late summer evening, shadow on the lawn enlarging

Into a mansion. The child gets it, enters.

Beginning with a Line by J.A.

Sunny things, the fins and buttons
Of childhood. Embroidered WWII patches.
Rock collection in egg carton. Prying
An orange section from the rind

With front teeth, no white residue.
Book at table, allowed when eating alone.
The arm socking game on the school bus.
Tar stuck to bare feet in summer.

Good Humor, Strawberry shortcake,
Chocolate Éclair. The taste of
Chlorinated water at the back of the throat.
Recess cruelty, circling the German

Exchange student: we the Spitfire
Fighter planes, spitting at him.
Lifting girl skirts, then running back
To our own. Did you see, what did you see?

The kid who was hemophiliac,
Never allowed out, the curtain-closed
Constancy of his bay window. All right, yes,
I see now: everything wasn't sunny;

To become memory, some things
Had to be lit from the inside. The guy in a cart,
Horse drawn, the slow clopping
Down our street. Misunderstanding

The words he called out—mournful
Repetition, a kind of singing. In the cart, a foot-
Pedaled stone wheel. Mother, holding out
Her drawer of knives for sharpening.

Beginning with a Line by Van Gogh

You take death to a star.
You shake a box of death and seeds fall out.
You swallow the 10:12 coming in to Grand Central.
You pull a fish spine from your throat.

You slip death a Benjamin, he spends it.
You hammer death's teeth, hammer breaks.
You recover, death stays.
You admire death's patience.

You down a shot of whiskey.
You sink through eons seamed with fossil.
You swim inches above the carbon-black sea floor.
You are blind, deaf. You are transparent.

For My Brother Who Couldn't Stay

In this poem one has taken the edge
Of one hand & swept the crumbs
From the counter.
In this poem we save
What falls & Jesus speaks lightly,
A breeze carrying the river's scent.
And all the day & night of this poem
A face asks what's left
After science, after the black & white
Movies, the forties camel hair coat, the nothing underneath.
The face in this poem asks & asks, and keeps
Asking, until Shut up, you want to say,
I'm sick of you & your
Permanent tears . . .
This poem looks out a cloudy porthole
At a branch-shaking tulip tree
Scratching to be let in.
And though this poem is a good swimmer
It can never be sure of reaching the equator, let alone
The dead-center self. Maybe,
If it could play the accordion in French,
After the war, that kind of sadness . . .
But this poem would rather be the wound than play it,
Would in fact widen the wound
So that we might take a deep breath & dolphin in

To the cooling blood, the salt river.
Lastly, this poem would like a word with you, Mother.
The word is: fallopian.
This poem, this difficulty with words—Mother, can you feel
The child beneath, breathing water?

Without God Everything is Permitted

I remember staring at a painting above
My crib: two swans on green water. But, to me
Shifting forms only. It's hard to see without words.
The less I talk to people, the less I want to.
    *

On an all-night car trip, I'm awakened
By the smell of coffee poured from mother's thermos
In the front seat, dark poured into dark. Later,
I burst from the theater into sun, and sneeze.
    *

You have a rich interior life, said the famous poet,
Then asked for a cigarette. A certain string
Of words makes a clack like billiards. My trunk
Of ghosts is shaking. I need a bigger trunk.
    *

A sigh takes in two times our usual breath.
Sigh again, sweet angel. On a pilgrimage to Innisfree
I swear I saw Yeats, standing on lake water.
I am a professor of the most useless art.

The Pearl

Helplessness will render us
The mollusk soft things we are.
We can choose to be that thing
With God, or without—
But we will never again be anything hard.
In a hallway glazed
Iridescent white, the scent
Of antiseptic, mixed with food
Cooling on steel racks.

The Truth About Men

I was around seven when mother found my drawing of a naked woman. Although I was hazy about female anatomy, I had recently surprised her as she came out of the shower. I deliberately made the drawing more baroque than necessary, adding lines and flourishes, especially to the breasts and pubis, which had become a mass of heavily inked black commas. My mother sat me down and placed the drawing before me on the kitchen table. "This is interesting," she said. "What is it a picture of?" "A machine," I answered. "Hmmm . . . it looks like a woman to me," she said, "a woman without her clothes. Is that it?" "No." She smiled at me and placed her hand on my head, then gently stroked my cheek. "It's all right if you've made a picture of a woman without her clothes," she said. "Is that what this is, a naked woman?" I looked away, out the kitchen window, at the weeping willow in our front yard. If you clipped a branch at just the right place and then stripped it of leaves it made an excellent whip. "It's ok. You can tell me." "No," I answered, knowing I would lie, as many times as I was asked, "It's a machine."

Shush

The women are calling out the men
& rightly so. I'm over here trying not to make noise.
I'm poor, the only sins I can afford
Are handmade. Mostly I watch TV. There, it's sex
& death—dawn to dusk. It's 3D desire in Dolby Atmos.
But, where is it not? I want
To climb in, into the confetti mass
Of electrons, to ululate among those golden mean
Faces, maybe snap one off like a virtual flower.

But mama said, You dasn't, you dasn't,
An imperative so whispery, so soft in the mouth
It almost seems unsounded, telepathic.
Mama's like everyone now—
In a home, she doesn't know where.
The saline bag's been needled, she's leaking out.

Anyway, it wasn't mama who said dasn't—
That was my Irish grandmother
Who died early, in a time when the terminal weren't told.
I lug the OED to the mahogany high desk & look—
Yep, the definition of mercy has changed.

But I remember seeing her before I went to college.
She knew, it was in her eyes. I knew she knew.

The Cloud

My mother's been dead for three months.
I don't know where she is now or how she got there.
I've heard all kinds of conjecture, and some
I believe. But first hand experience comes last.

Soon, I'm going on vacation to Florida,
A state she lived in many years. She loved the sun
And would lie for hours in its glossy lacquer.
Later on she preferred to stay indoors.

Quatrains are useful because, as Creeley
Said: strong feeling wants a container.
At least, I remember words to that effect.
All words mingle, eventually, in the same cloud.

I also like Florida, the ocean more than the sun.
Being in waves reminds me of something
I once was, and maybe will be again.
But I have no idea, really, what I mean by that.

Satin

The edge of non-being nudges me.
It's smooth as the satin lining a coffin.
Some absences don't signify. I lack
wings, for example, but am

content to walk beneath
a sky often generous—sun in leaves
a thousand shades of green.
They fan, they shift and glitter.

I don't get negative space.
I prefer the branches it contains.
I have taken reasonable care of the body.
I have left room for meat and sugar.

This moment and every other,
like strips of torn satin—
they flutter, tied to a fence
running back to Buffalo, New York.

Blurb Cento

Nothing one can say
Sweeps up a life and fixes it

the way lightning or heartbreak do.
To speak is to be horrified.

The unadorned, the skeletal,
The disembodied voice of a mother

Shot through with regard—
Love building its house.

Her sternness reminds us
The voice brims

To be understood, even missed.
We never get enough.

If you count yourself
Among the unredeemed

Afraid of loneliness, of what
Happens after death

What you need is distraction,
The paradoxical snap

When things come together.
This book shoulders

The entire sky, this book emits light.
It will change you.

2022

Ah you, poems, you're no help.
You balance on the edge of a balcony and then, nothing.
Nothing happens.

And the wheels in the sky and the wheels in the earth
Are also imagined, though I can't say
What's really there.

My neighbor's blue and yellow flag,
Does it help? We like to think. But how, poem? Unless thought
Somehow turn gas to solid, wish to treaty.

I've been expecting too much of creation. It's only
A huge child playing marbles
On the periodic table, itself made of the table.

Ah you, poems, you're no help—
You balance on the edge of a balcony, ghost or gargoyle.
You peel an apple. You swallow the sun.

II

In the Mind

In the mind of trees we are a general blur.
In the mind of mountains we lack density, we are falling.
In the mind of pavement we are mild without wheels, easily borne.
In the mind of Paris we can do whatever. Paris could care less.

The ghost of Portofino, eating tiny octopi on the moon,
Motioned me to join his table. The sea a dusty blue,
Centuries showing through layered rock. I remember
That day like it was my whole life, that day it was.

See-through language is a threat to power.
Power wants it densely woven, without slub or seam—
The same Kevlar worn ten thousand years. I shouted this
From a condo balcony, and was instantly ignored.

In the mind of train stations we are radiant mourners.
In the mind of deserts, lassoed streams.
In the minds of men, women, in all times all places: god.
In the mind of scarab beetles: tall, rich food.

Sober Ghost

Thirty years since I've come down from a high. Something like falling down a flight of stairs, as I recall. I mean, the latter stages. In the beginning it's just a greased slide to the foot of the next high. At that point you can eat donuts for breakfast every morning and nothing happens. Your autocorrect functions, perfectly.

Hey dad, what's the weather like at your mountain home? Can you ski, can you swim, can you joke? Have you found out how much of what we see here is a screen, placed in front of something else? I've often suspected drunkenness is behind trees bending furiously in the wind, for example. Speaking of booze, are you glad you stepped off the planet sober?

I ask these questions half expecting a mouth to materialize in the air and answer. I myself don't have much to report. As far as I can tell my own soul has been getting thinner. At this point it's a sheen beneath my loosening skin. When I wake at night and walk a few yards into the dark my body glows, slightly. Almost enough to see.

***How He Was Caught Up into Paradise, and Heard
Unspeakable Words, which It Is Not Lawful
for a Man to Utter***

One thing I may not speak of
Is the idea that saved my life. It's not that
The idea's forbidden, nor the name,
Which many of the saved
Call divine, it's that speaking on behalf of idea
Comingles it with the speaker's will
Diluting both, and when the next
Frayed-to-bare-wire human receives the signal
Salvation's siphoned off
By the speaker's self-love, and all is lost.
Nevertheless, I want to talk
About the idea, for I have seen it in the flesh,
Seen it work through embodiment
In those who came before—
Resurrection from cellular despair, the body
Thrown down from a great height
To the maggot canyon, the groundless floor,
Then pulled up shining newborn by angelic hands.
But I have also seen it fail
To permeate many who I loved,
Who one night embraced me, and the next
Put gun to mouth and divorced all creation, excepting
The invisible. Nor can I say why,
Why them, not me. Nor can anyone.

I'm Thinking of a Few Spectacular Ways to Die

If it's not about something, what is it about. The trees brush close to reply but suddenly it's fall and they drop everything. Now I can see through the forest to the far brown slope. Maybe I'll build a zip line. My father when he began aging talked more and more about the dangerous things he wanted to do—parasail, wingsuit, piano lessons. Modes of flight. I'd like to chat with him now, but he's dead. We are closer than ever. And my favorite bird, the pileated woodpecker, has also disappeared. It's a bird with calls and drumming but no song. I miss his oversize body hanging upside down from the feeder, the jackhammer of his red and black head, stabbing at seed.

Homage to Phil

I don't know what you know about work
But I can tell you this: thinking is easier. You get up,
Put on your head and there you are.
Whereas, when dawn settles on the factory
You take that gray chill inside
And it stays. Muscle wakes machine, and both
Flex together the same way three thousand times.
Then someone else mops another day
From polished concrete floors.
I'm not saying it's hard, I'm saying
My Portuguese landlord had a beautiful face
And when I climbed the stairs onions were frying
And a language with no sharp edges
Came from behind his door, Jeffrey,
He'd call, Come, have wine! But I had serious drinking
Of my own to do and smiled and said
Thanks, not tonight. After the third drink
The onions faded from my shirt,
My head blossomed into book and cheap cigar,
And Claudius, the bastard who killed the father, trumpeted
Into the room, demanding obedience.
And, though I knew none of it was real
I also heard the woman inside the carriage making love
To a fool. The horse snorted, the carriage flew
Through my kitchen, then down the drain of night.

(Words) (Music) (Money)

Somehow, I got lost on the way to work.
But look—the brochure of mountain train rides has arrived!
You can peruse a book of pictures, but it feels wrong.
Is it possible to see words without reading them?

"Welcome!" he said, and swept back his arm majestically.
That's my thing, there—the nature of words in extremis.
The pandemic removed a section of bone from the child's leg.
When I imagine my own death, the picture goes static.

I have retired my ambitions to a field. They chew, roundly, like cows.
I was concerned too many of us packed into the vaporetto.
Worries about children sink to the lake's silt floor.
I listen to your song, but can't wait till you hear mine.

I get excited about calling distant friends, then don't.
I dream someone has stolen my patents. Or, maybe, parents.
One foot in the boat and one on the dock, boat easing out.
I know some people still use them, but I miss stamps.

Worries about children rise out of the mud and walk home.
The hard plastic packaging cost me a bloodied hand.
There's something profound in stone soup, she said, adding carrots.
I scooped up the word *lanugo*, polished it, put it in my pocket.

As a child, the stack of Horizon magazines had great value.
Politicians are once more pretending to club each other, until
    We bruise.
My most recent find, a bone necklace: *nomenclature*.
The path of thought is smooth, without the clack of digital gates.

I remember one family drive when I could suddenly read the signs,
    My lonely power.
People much prefer a house built of music over one of words.
Words would be music, if they didn't mean.
There are no words in money.

Insomnia

Walking the Mobius strip, sleep just up ahead, on the other side. I have a strong sense of self, which I lose track of easily and often. The dark gets all up in my face. I can see a little through my daughter, but most of the future's socked in by fog. Thoughts, lost before I can write them down. Yes, I'll have those thoughts again in the next world and yes, some will still be stupid. If salvation depended on the social life, I'd be damned. My mother keeps asking to go home. But when I ask what home, she can't say where, or when. At some point everyone whispers, OK *death, show me what you got.*

The Nighthawk

I go back to warn the guy I used to be. But when I get there he looks tired, eating alone in the diner. He's just come from the four-to-twelve shift. I can't bring myself to touch his arm, or speak. Besides, it's clear I'm not much of anything to him—a spot of ketchup on his tie, a shadow passing through the parking lot. He chews, looking straight ahead, beer in hand, cigarettes and zippo on the Formica counter. And still so much night left to go.

The Afterlife Has Already Begun

You know that complicated sky with porticoes and cliff dwellings and municipalities of clouds, and aureate shafts plunging like glory to light moving patches of earth below, and in another section of the 360 a hundred thousand starlings twisting inside-out on a blue panel, or funneling through a bright nick in the cloud's flank, and you, watching from the cubby beneath the curved rear window of the VW—that impossible, ruddy, inflated rhetoric of a sky? Yes, yes of course you know.

*

You can wait a long time, and will. It was back in the day you couldn't comprehend the thought that things were going along normally. What could such a thing mean? Actually, it might have been of some help, that thought. Your fear preferred to apply an electrical charge directly to the nerve's root. Maybe if I cover myself with clothes similar to the others I will be passed over, you thought. And the tube tilted to keep the electrode away from the drawn-out end, melted off, then fastened to the next in line.

*

You don't need to dress up anymore, that part's well gone. Still, you suspect mother waits for you, somewhere. You'd go shopping together in the Husky Boy section, in that itchy fucking yellow sweater with the bear on it. That you, mom? No—just a few crumbs falling to an old man's shirt. Seems right, mother's made of food, doesn't it? Mmmm. And father, metal. I guess. And you, torn between foundry and kitchen. Definitely. On the other hand, a leather apron is not only protective, but everywhere appropriate.

*

In the afterlife all the houses you've lived in are gathered together in one uncomfortable block. It's like some kind of intelligence test, picking up each house and turning it, to see where it fits. But you can also whisper—for example, *Surface of the moon*—and feel the immediate gray silt underfoot, see the crisp shadowed light. Maybe we'll meet there, and exchange stories of the sweet parts. Which means: live them again, this time without fear. Or, maybe I'll just smile and turn over in my sleep.

Mission Creep

When I woke my cross was turned wrong side out, silver to the world, gold inward. Must have been some dream I can't remember, one from the genre of tumult and fire and whipped up clouds.

*

Art can do many things—sit, roll over, speak, piss. Even atone. We prefer shock and awe, of course, which doesn't make it right, or left, above or below. Only an auction house thinks art is worth what it costs to make, or buy. Only demons short the futures of song. The huge wood sculpture in Chelsea continuously changed shape, but so slowly you couldn't tell—the basic material remained the same—until it had become a different thing entirely. I liked that.

*

When my father retired he no longer understood the mission. This drive to the post office, I could see him thinking, this isn't really a big deal. But I was still engaged, and did not then understand the look on his face.

*

The philosopher opened his briefcase and took out a sheaf of papers and placed it on the lectern, squaring the corners. The subject of tonight's talk is free will, he began. First we must distinguish what we mean by free, and what we mean by will. They are not words, but rather, flighty angels or abstractions, and must be brought to ground. Then we will discuss the new thing made by putting these freshly clipped wings together, and how that coupling affects the valence on either side, if you will. Then we'll grab free, and will, bind them to the bed, and drain each of blood and plasma. Then scrub, until we can see clean through and they squeak, each of them separately, as we run a dry finger across their surfaces. We will posit god, and situate these terms within god's body, and see if god sneezes or chokes or looks askance, or pauses even slightly in his step on the way to the next essential engagement. Then remove god and see if free will can survive an otherwise empty universe. Finally, we will add one man—and one man only—and attempt to track with as much precision and solicitude as we may, the ensuing chaos. Good night, I'll say, in hopes that all of us leave the theater and journey home in silence, and sit a moment in the inmost room of our inmost house, and think, drink in hand or not, about the infinite delicate atrocities we have committed. Thank you for coming. You needn't have.

*

Damien Hirst found an 18th century skull in a shop in Islington and paid to have it sectioned, cast in platinum, and reassembled. Then had the original teeth installed in the platinum skull, and hired jewelers to embed 8,601 diamonds, completely covering its surface. Finally, a pear-shaped pink diamond called Skull Star was placed in the center of the bejeweled forehead. "Celestial, almost" said a critic. Before the exhibit opening, Hirst took his mother to the gallery. "What will you do next, for the love of God?" she said. It was shown in an illuminated glass case, in darkened rooms.

After a world tour—with stops in Amsterdam, Florence, London, Doha, and Oslo—*For the Love of God* sold for one hundred million pounds.

*

My father sat in a floating pool of light reading my poems. It was his actual chair, his lamp, my book. But all else in his living room had been erased, green-screened out. He was suspended inside a globe of stars and his local position was total darkness, except for the lamp. As we know, it is difficult to tell both direction and momentum without a point of reference—impossible, really. To me he appeared to be floating, though it might have been we were moving in the same direction at the same velocity. Or, both of us were stationary. What do you think? I asked him. He lowered his reading glasses and closed the book. It's good, what I understand of it, he said. My only regret is that you never joined Rotary. We really needed more people like you. With that he readjusted his glasses and went back to reading.

*

Something mute and woodsy intrudes: the bamboo branch with its clutch of spear-point feathers, swiping slowly down the dining room window.

*

I fell into the cross long ago. Then, was born. I'm talking about the cross at the center of the universe, the portal through which everyone enters. If you can't sign on, I understand. I myself often wake up, thinking—it's such a simple story, OMG! You really have to be an idiot, or a child. And then I ready myself once more, with determined look, ankle holstered M-1911, extra magazines, Kevlar skin, push-dagger-neck-knife, and my awesome, shimmering desire. Brothers and sisters, metaphor has covered us all with a light snow. It is everything we see and feel. But, here, take my literal hands. Put them somewhere next to your body and keep them with you, please. They are so cold, my literal hands.

I Said to My Friend Jimmy

I said to my friend Jimmy it's a different world
I said to Sarah how about a zip line in the back yard?
I said to my daughters any minute now comes the reversal
To my friend Dick I said Hey, no answer, he's dead

I knelt in the serotonin shower after sex
I knelt in the news till one patella fell off, then the other
I knelt to God and he said I know, I know . . .
I knelt in things, bewitched, surrounded by things!

I pet the dog she looks up at me
I pet my car it's alive in a stupid manner
I pet an ant it enlarges into a black Lamborghini
I pet my ambitions, such tall eager sons

Jimmy says he makes money flipping houses
Jimmy says let them come, who gives a fuck
Jimmy says beauty is its own justification

On the Anniversary of My Sobriety

Sam could cry, but
Could not stay sober. His job: a headset
Telephone, a script. Easy. Easy if
You can't stay sober. Sam hoarded
Years for his Hawaiian trip,
His salvation.

Stepping from the plane
Big warm push of air—salt & plumeria alba,
Sea the color of Julie Christie's eyes.

The hotel room
Phone brought booze, food,
DVDs. The flat screen
Black & deep. Sam inserted Dr. Zhivago
& did not leave. Packets of macadamia nuts
On pillow. Maid to lust after.

Then, Sam died &
Carol died, & Ed, Kareem, Philip & Betsy died, Seamus,
Old Ms. Blankenbaker, & the sea
Of unnamed who could cry
But not stay sober.

Brothers & sisters, it was nothing I did.

Something opened my face & I cried, then stood, & followed
The love that bought this world.

River, Bear

Been swimming the river
within the river, song of skin
touched and left humming.
Been flying over the past,
no sound but dry husk
of wind. Been landing
at intervals to embrace
mother, father, earth
family gone but breathing
in me still. Been pitching
our tent in forest, bear
rampant outside the flap—
that fear, always. All
right then: that's a wrap.
That's a life. Now to wake
happy in the river's
scent, to wake singing
like there's no tomorrow,
bear gone, gone for good.

Prospero's Happiness

I was a piece of music pinned to the horizon
No, I was me sitting in a wooden chair
All sorts of furious thoughts collapse
When you're not looking
There was the wall
I punched three holes to let what was left
Of the marriage escape
If you're human there's no escape
You have to be human
Leave me alone about the new sins
Every one of them is ancient and familiar
Still I feel useless and shamed
When it's only the spell
Of the new poem holding me in its arms
And why am I not out there saving the world, etc.
That's culture for you
But I can't help it
Nothing beats a squealing newborn poem
In your arms, all wet and huge-eyed
I could have been a successful scat singer
On Neptune I think
For all they know about scat singing on Neptune
On this planet everybody knows
Everything about everything
Except how it began

And what's the damn reason for it anyhow
Sometimes I think I'd be all right
Alone, but no I need people it's proven by science
Nevertheless I took a picture
Of an island and
Enhanced my solitary presence there
With Photoshop
A trick I learned on YouTube
Of course when God
Does it you really are enhanced
The fruit trees laden
The coconuts filled with milk and white meat
And this is in fact the place
I have come to rest—
Prospero surveying his island
From a mesh hammock
Plush sky, stars and planets embossed
A garden, blue ocean, my wife
And daughters close enough to hear me sigh—
Child of God eating an orange in the sun

The Lion

You coat yourself in petroleum.
You slap your own face at the thought.
You throw sticks at the snake in your path.
You crack open a golden egg.

You stuff a hundred in the kettle.
You yearn for a phone with black heft.
You watch snow falling in the past.
You no longer dance, alone, so crazy!

You thread through crowded rooms.
You batten down, you fly upright.
You gather fragments of gold shell.
You have lost the one most proud.

You no longer bait or tease the lion.
You feed the lion. You keep him ready.

It Was Later

It was later and, after that, later still.
It was the smell of dead mouse in the wall.
Its hands were tied, alarming the guests.

Its name is legion. It desires you.
It's the boy fallen through ice.
It's the echoing field between particles.

It's age, and the deaths, and the ghosts.
It's a rodent scuttling through walls.
It's the burnt toast smell of outer space.

It's a Bariloche from my collection of hats.
It's the boy, tempting the surface.
It's a red line through everyone I love.

It's age, the more of it the less to spend.
It's desire they tell us to be rid of.
No. It's desire that says, I live.

Bearing Away

Thirty years from drink
No one can call
Pain useless.
Tide fills the inlet
Of your arms,
Ball, socket, childlike
Sun and moon
Held close. Your
Mind backs up, a steel
Propeller
In reverse. Which,
Then, what part
Was sailing?
Dusk a burnt
Orange haze
Of self, boat, sea,
Planet—standing still.
Jib stowed,
Moor lines thrown.
You feel
With one foot
For the dock—planks
Rough hewn
From new heaven,
New earth.

Even Night is Not Night Enough

For I woke with a walnut for a skull
For every star switched on, burning through black pages
For if you seek God you will find His children
For everything I know fits in a walnut
For every scene I once lived now invisible

For I didn't want to meet people but my eyes were forced open
For I reach around back of me for a weapon
For those I hurt stand before me in a long line
For I am radiation like the sun
For the sun doesn't love us, love is a hundred floors beneath
For I wish to get off there, please

For I have no hometown and never did
For I carry my box of crayons into the void
For I remember the willow teasing with silky wave
For when you break open night there is a walnut and another
    Night inside that
For I will never be prepared for paradise

For money is a strong contender
For I admire Rotarians from the cover of a different language
For stars are sleep God rubs from His eyes
For I lifted my children overhead so they could see
For I have never understood parades

For there are whisperings in the mansion's shadow
For I cut my shadow out of concrete and took it with me
For what is the point of being visible if not dancing
For I don't dance
For I dance on a tiny stage inside the walnut
For the children I shoo from my lawn belong to me
For Kahlil Gibran was wrong about children

For the universe is a species of hydraulic thought
For I remember the teacher who blessed me and the teacher who
 Failed me
For human current alternates between praise and humiliation
For when I plug in the music is loud metal
For panic has become our default

For I still have wishes but they fit in a bullet casing
For I am ocean blood
For I thought a brain would serve but it's only a franchise
For the point is sober, more Amish than Vegas
For God is fearful pissed off
For we cannot descend to the depths of His mercy

For my wife's talisman is mountain, mine sea
For I have only recently occupied the whole of my body
For I am wonderous made
For my hands drift up in zero gravity, purest black
For my feet take me so far, no farther
For the bruise on my side contains galaxies

For my ancestors trace back to a man drawing a man
For my children ricochet close to the bone
For my skull is a shell, the basin of existence

ACKNOWLEDGEMENTS

The American Journal of Poetry: "On the Anniversary of my Sobriety," "Wingsuit"

The American Poetry Review: "In the Mind," "Even Night is Not Night Enough"

Bennington Review: "Fronting"

Diagram: "My Lion"

Disclaimer Magazine (UK): "The Channel Swimmer"

FENCE: "I Said to My Friend Jimmy"

Ploughshares: "For My Brother Who Couldn't Stay"

The Los Angeles Review: "Insomnia," "The Nighthawk"

Lucent Dreaming: "River, Bear"

Michigan Quarterly Review: "Shush," "The Truth About Men," "Fields"

Mockingbird: "Lack of Perspective in an Early Drawing by One of My Daughters," "The Pearl"

New England Review: "Love & Judgment"

North American Review: "Homage to Phil", The Afterlife Has Already Begun,", "Without God Everything is Permitted"

[PANK]: "A Marriage," "It Was Later"

The Paris Review: "The Cloud," "The Mansion"

The Southern Review: "I'm Thinking of a Few Spectacular Ways to Die"

The Threepenny Review: "Motion Against Ideas"

Under a Warm Green Linden: "Prospero's Happiness"

Volt: "(Words) (Music) (Money)"

"Mission Creep" won first prize in *Lucent Dreaming*'s contest for flash fiction, 2021. "River, Bear" was also published in *Lucent Dreaming* print anthology titled Hope Is the Thing.

NOTES

"Beginning with a Line by J.A.": the title refers to John Ashbery, and was inspired by his poem, "Picture of Little J.A. in a Prospect of Flowers."

"It Was Later": the line "age, and the deaths, and the ghosts," is lifted from a poem by John Berryman.

"Even Night is not Night Enough": the title is a phrase from a letter by Kafka.

"How He Was Caught Up into Paradise, and Heard Unspeakable Words, which It Is Not Lawful for a Man to Utter": 2 Corinthians 12:4, KJV (altered slightly).

ABOUT THE AUTHOR

Poet, playwright, and essayist Jeffrey Skinner was awarded a 2014 Guggenheim Fellowship in Poetry. Skinner's Guggenheim project involved a conflation of contemporary physics, poetry, and theology, and he served as the June, 2015 Artist in Residence at the CERN particle accelerator in Geneva, Switzerland. In 2015 he was awarded one of eight American Academy of Arts & Letters Awards, for exceptional accomplishment in writing. His writing has also been awarded grants and fellowships from such sources as the National Endowment for the Arts, The Ingram Merrill Foundation, and the Howard Foundation. He's been the beneficiary of residencies at Yaddo, McDowell, Vermont Studios, and the Fine Arts Center in Provincetown, and served as Poet-in-Residence at the James Merrill House in Connecticut, the Frost House in New Hampshire, and the Arts Festival in Kildare County, Ireland.

His most recent prose book, *The 6.5 Practices of Moderately Successful Poets*, was published to wide attention and acclaim, including a full page review in the *Sunday New York Times Book Review*. He has edited two anthologies, *Last Call: Poems of Alcoholism, Addiction, and Deliverance*; and *Passing the Word: Poets and Their Mentors*. Skinner's poems have appeared in many magazines, including *The New Yorker, The Atlantic, The Nation, The American Poetry Review, Poetry, FENCE, Bomb, VOLT*, and *The Paris Review*.

With his wife Sarah Gorham, Skinner cofounded Sarabande Books, which won the inaugural AWP Small Press Publisher Award, and the Golden Colophon Award from CLMP. He is Professor Emeritus at The University of Louisville.

JEFFREY SKINNER